# ISLA AND LULU

## NOËLLE GENTILE

ILLUSTRATIONS

MARIA G. GAMA

**T**hank you for the endless love from all of the members of Team Isla. Thank you Mom and Dad (Deborah and Daniel Gentile) and our family and friends, the Saturday Night Crew, Taina Asili, Jonathan Ashley, Susan Alexrod, Jennifer Bartels, Lily Bartels, Karen Berstein, Leora Berstein, Nathan Bogardus, Melissa Browning, Kathleen Carey, Alisa Sikelianos-Carter, Judi Corvinelli, Star Corvinelli, Olaiya Curtis, Ward Dales, Erica DiNicola, Amanda Gentile, Amanda Green, Lori Kidd, Astrid Killikelly, Clenard Killikelly, Christina King, Jason Litwak, Marguerite Lodico, Loretta Longo, Gregory Theodore Marsh, Aaron Moore, Jamel Mosely, Angie Nelson, Robert O'Hare, Lindsey Pensabene, Jessica Phillips, Dr. Annapurna Poduri, Michael Premo, Dr. Tammy Ellis-Robinson, Matt Ryan, Bhawin Suchak, Julie Sullivan, Leah Threatte, Gaetano Vaccaro and Johanna Voutounou, for your support, guidance and encouragement in creating this book, our story.

A special thank you to David Heredia for lighting the path forward and to Maria Gabriela Gama for bringing our story to life with your beautiful illustrations.

**Title**
Isla and Lulu

**Author**
Noëlle Gentile

**Illustrator**
Maria Gabriela Gama

**Layout Designer**
Maria Gabriela Gama

**Editing support**
Taina Asili, Jennifer Bartels, Lily Bartels, Jackie Bogardus, Nathan Bogardus, Melissa Browning, Alisa Sikelianos-Carter, Amanda Green, Kim Farquharson Kelly, Astrid Killikelly, Clenard Killikelly, Loretta Longo, Angie Nelson, Lindsey Pensabene, Leah Threatte, Gaetano Vaccaro and Johanna Voutounou

**Autism Spectrum Disorder Infographic Content**
Loretta Longo

**Epilepsy Infographic Content**
Erica DiNicola

**Content Consultant**
Lindsey Pensabene

......................................................

Printed in the United States of America

First Printing, 2019

ISBN 978-1-7923-1538-1

For Isla, Lucia and Nathan.
I'm so thankful we get to ride the waves together.
**I love you, always.**

# Our Family's Story

Thank you for joining us on our journey! We hope you enjoy reading our story.

In October of 2015, Isla had her first seizure. In February of 2016, after enduring a prolonged seizure in which she was treated in ICU, Isla was diagnosed with Epilepsy.

It wasn't until our family began doing research on **the link between autism and epilepsy** that we decided to have Isla tested for autism. In June of 2017, Isla was diagnosed on the **autism spectrum**. Our family was very lucky to get a relatively early diagnosis for Isla. She was 5 years old. Girls often go undiagnosed for longer than boys, often times being misdiagnosed with conditions that mimic autism. Having both of these diagnoses has been life-changing for the ways we have been able to support and advocate for Isla.

Isla and Lucia are not only sisters, **they are best friends.** We love our life together. We have had such a great adventure that has brought us to the most beautiful peaks and some of the deepest valleys. We've all learned so much about ourselves and each other along the way.

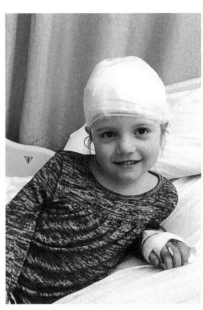

A dear friend told us, "Isla doesn't need to change for the world, the world needs to change for Isla."

We hope by sharing our story with you that we will be one small part of making the world a more loving and inclusive place. It is our greatest wish that you and your loved ones feel seen, celebrated and loved for exactly who you are, especially by those closest to you.

My name is Lucia, which means light, but everyone calls me Lulu.

This is Isla Kai,
her name means Island
in the Sea.

Isla was born on a hot April day.
My dad says just before Isla was born,
he and mommy were racing up the
West Side Highway in a taxi.

My mom says when Isla was born,
the New York City skyline sparkled
just for her.

I was born as the December snow fell and my mom says it was like we were in our own little snow globe together.

My dad says he was so proud to drive me home from the hospital but also a little scared because the snow was piled so high on the ground.

It's the four of us: Mom, Dad, Isla and me!

My family does lots of fun things together, but our most favorite thing to do is go to the beach!

We play in the sand and water all day long.

Sometimes, Mom and Dad turn us into mermaids in the sand.

Isla is my big sister. I love her and she loves me.

Isla is on the autism spectrum. My mom says it means her brain works a little differently from mine.

Sometimes other people don't understand Isla or how she's feeling. But Isla and I understand each other.

I know she loves me when she hugs and kisses me. Isla saves her hugs and kisses for when she really wants to give them, so I know they are special.

I know she's happy
when she laughs her big
belly laugh.

I know she's sad when
her tears sit like
puddles in her eyes.

I know she's angry
when she "grrrs" like
a tiger.

I know she's excited
when her eyes light up
and she clasps her hands
around her face.

Isla is really funny.
Sometimes we roll around on the
floor together, hugging each other
and laughing.

Sometimes I play the games Isla
likes to play, like putting her
cards in and out of the box or
pretending to be camping.

When I'm hurt, Isla always runs over to me
with an ice pack and a hug to take care of me.

Sometimes Isla takes apart my puzzle while I'm putting it together. She wants to put the pieces in the box. That makes me feel frustrated. But dad reminds me that sometimes I take Isla's toys from her too.

Sometimes Isla has seizures
because she also has epilepsy.

My mom says the medicine that Isla takes to stop
her from having more seizures makes it hard
for her to control herself.

Do you know what a seizure is?
I didn't either.

It's like lightning flashing
through your brain.

When Isla has a seizure I get really scared.

My mommy and daddy are really scared too. Isla can't talk to us, she stares off to the side and sometimes her body shakes.

Mommy and Daddy have to give her a special medicine to make her seizure stop.

So much is happening,
it's like we're in a little boat in the
middle of a stormy sea with waves
crashing all around us.

I hold on to Mommy really tight because I'm so worried.

The firefighters and ambulance come to take Isla to the hospital.

I wish I could go to the hospital with Isla but I have to stay home.

I worry about her when she's in the hospital. I try to be brave like Isla.

I pretend I am a news reporter
interviewing Isla about what it's like
to be in a hospital!

Even though I'm little,
I have really big feelings.
I don't always know what to
do with them.

Sometimes I pretend my dollies are having seizures and I take care of them.

I know Isla is always happy when she comes home.
I feel so proud of her.

Isla is my big sister and we take care of each other. Our friends take care of us too. They play with Isla in her way and with me in my way.

I don't ever want anyone to leave her out because she's different. If someone needs help figuring out the best way to play with Isla, I'm there to help.

Isla teaches me things and
I teach Isla things.

Isla taught me that being different is amazing.

She likes to say,
"This is me. I'm Isla."

I may be little, but I love Isla
in really big ways.

We may be little, but we are making the world a better place for Isla and all of the kids whose brains and bodies work a little differently.

I love Isla,
my island in
the sea.

# Autism Spectrum Disorder

## Do you know what having a disability means?

It means being different than most people, in a way that may make certain activities more difficult. Different doesn't mean wrong, or less important. Autism Spectrum Disorder is one disability.

## 1 in 59 babies are born autistic.

(CDC, 2014)

Their parents may notice that they are a little different from most babies by the time they are **1 year old. Usually by 2**, parents are asking doctors for help with understanding what is different about their child. **By age 3-4** most parents learn that their child is autistic and they start to learn more about autism spectrum disorder and how to best support their children. However, many people get a diagnosis later in life, especially girls.

If you meet a friend who is autistic, there is nothing to be afraid of. Autism isn't an illness or disease and isn't contagious.

**Autistic people are people just like you.**

## Why do autistic children act differently from me?

Some autistic kids may (Autism Society, 2017):

• Have trouble talking, make strange sounds, or not talk at all; or they may flap their hands, spin, or laugh a lot.

Just because some autistic people may not be able to use their own words, it does not mean they can't understand your words. Please talk to them as you do with your other friends. Instead of words, some autistic people may use actions to express their feelings.

For example, when they are excited or happy, they may flap their hands, jump up and down, or run in circles. Or they may do all these things at once to help them calm down or to help them process what's going on around them. This is called "stimming".

• Sit quietly and not look at others.

However, this does not mean you should stop trying to talk to them. Your friends can hear and understand you. It just helps them to listen fully by looking away and not making eye contact.

• Play or behave differently from other friends;

- Be very active or very quiet and like to spend time alone;

- Have trouble looking directly at you; or

- Do or say the same things over and over again (like lining up toys or repeating a line from a movie).

**When you have an autistic friend, you both learn a lot from each other. Here are some ways to be a great friend (Autism Society, 2017):**

- Accept your friend's differences.

- Celebrate your friend for who they are!

- Protect your friend from things that bother them.

Some autistic children may not see, hear, or feel things the same way you do. Some noises that don't bother you may hurt their ears. Some may have trouble eating certain foods because of the way they taste and feel. Others may be very sensitive to certain smells. On the other hand, things that may bother you, like a bee sting, may not appear to be as painful to them.

Protect your friend when others try to bully or make them do something that is not appropriate. It is hard for some autistic children to understand what we say or what our facial and body expressions mean.

For example, if you are frowning, your autistic classmate may not be able to understand that you are sad.

- Use pictures or write down what you want to say to help your friend understand.

- Join your friend in activities that interest them.

- Be patient. Wait; give them extra time to answer your question or complete an activity.

- Invite your friend to play with you and to join you in group activities. Teach your friend the rules by showing them what to do in an activity or game.

- Sit near your friend whenever you can, and help them do things if they want you to.

Do not assume that your autistic friends can't do something, simply because they are autistic. Ask if you can help them, but do not just do things for them – unless you have their permission. You like the feeling of succeeding and your autistic friends do too!

- Help other kids learn about autism.

## It's important to remember:

Some autistic people do not feel that they have a disorder and don't want to be anything different from who they are. While they may have different strengths or weaknesses than other people, they are proud of who they are and they deserve acceptance. Autistic people are born exactly the way they are supposed to be born, just like you. There is nothing wrong with autistic people, just like there is nothing wrong with you.

# Seizures and Epilepsy

Reviewed by Erica DeNicola-Scher, MS, Director of Community Education and Advocacy Coordinator for the Epilepsy Foundation of North-eastern New York.

it can change the way you think, how you feel, or make your body do things that you can't control.

• Seizures do not hurt, but a person might feel scared when a seizure happens and might not feel well after a seizure is over.

• Most seizures last only a few seconds or a few minutes. But some people, like Isla, have seizures that last longer than five minutes. If a seizure lasts longer than five minutes, call 911 because special medicine and treatment are needed.

## Things to remember about seizures and epilepsy:

About **1 in 4** autistic children also have **epilepsy**.

• You can't catch epilepsy from someone who has it, and you can't give it to someone else if you have it.

• If you have seizures, you are not alone. Lots and lots of other children have epilepsy too. In fact, more than 65 million people have epilepsy worldwide.

• There are lots of different kinds of seizures. More than twenty!

• Seizures begin in the network of cells that make up your brain. When you are having a seizure,

## What to do if a seizure happens:

• Send someone to find a grown up.

• If the person is on the ground and shaking, help turn the person to their side. Put something small and soft under their head.

• Move anything that could hurt them out of the way.

• If they are walking around, stay with them. If you are inside, shut the door and let them walk in the room with you. Understand that they may not be able to understand what you say to them during the seizure.

• As the seizure ends, sit down with them until a grown up comes.

• Be a friend when the seizure is done.

# What you should never do if a seizure happens:

- Never try to hold on to or restrain a person during a seizure.

- Never put anything in a person's mouth during a seizure.

- Never leave alone a person having a seizure.

- Never tease someone or poke fun at someone who has had a seizure.

# References

**"Growing Up Together"** and **"Growing Up Together** – Teens with Autism". Autism Society of America. Retrieved from: https://www.autism-society.org/wp-content/uploads/2017/12/Growing-Up-Together-Elementary-2017R.pdf and https://www.autism-society.org/wp-content/uploads/2017/04/GrowingupTeens-updated-2017.pdf

**"What is Autism"** Retrieved from https://www.autism-society.org/wp-content/uploads/2014/04/What_is_Autism_Final.pdf

**1 in 59 statistic** Retrieved from: https://www.cdc.gov/ncbddd/autism/addm.html

**"What if my friend has Autism Spectrum Disorder?"**, Dr. Diane E. Treadwell-Deering. Retrieved from: https://kidshealth.org/en/kids/autism.html#.XQbvsogvHZE.email

Noëlle Gentile

**Noëlle Gentile** is a director, producer, writer and artist educator, who seeks to create spaces for people to tell their stories through writing, film and theatre as a vehicle for transformation, healing and connection. She lives in upstate New York with her family.

Maria Gabriela

**Maria Gabriela Gama** is a Brazilian graphic designer and illustrator. She is involved with multiple children-related projects and hopes to promote positive changes through her art.